PIANO • VOCAL • GUITAR

SANTA'S
GREATEST HITS

ISBN 0-634-08203-5

HAL•LEONARD® CORPORATION

7777 W. BLUEMOUND RD. P.O. BOX 13819 MILWAUKEE, WI 53213

Visit Hal Leonard Online at
www.halleonard.com

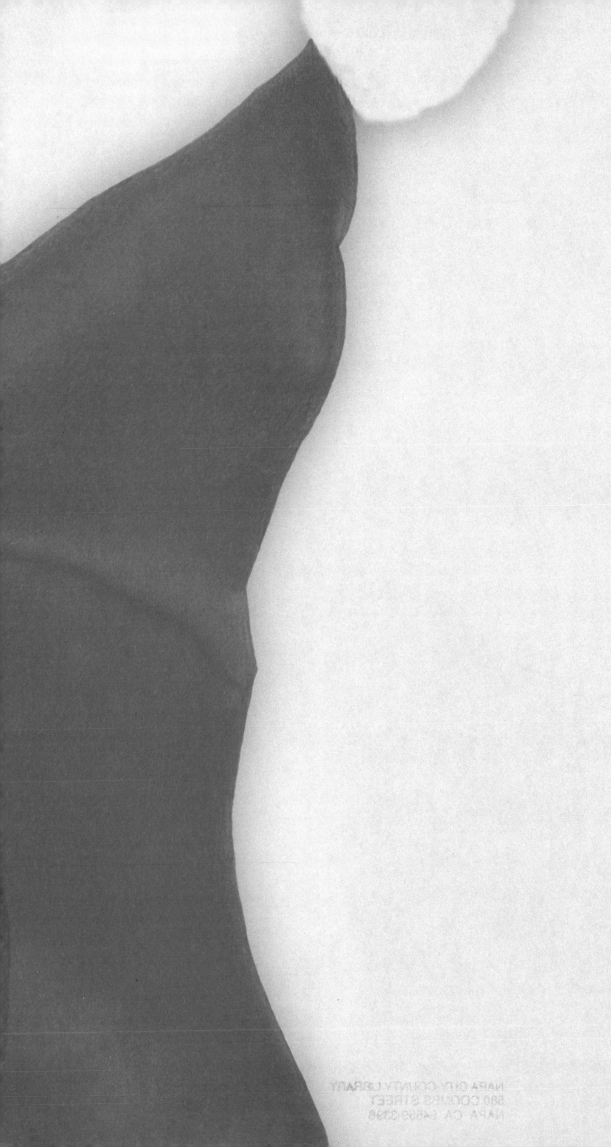

C O N T E N T S

4 Blue Christmas

6 Brazilian Sleigh Bells

16 Caroling, Caroling

18 The Chipmunk Song

13 Christmas Day

20 Christmas Is

23 A Christmas Memory

28 Christmas Time Is Here

31 Do You Hear What I Hear

34 Feels Like Christmas

39 Frosty the Snow Man

42 Give Thanks

47 God Bless My Family

52 Grandma's Spending Christmas with the Superstars

59 Grown-Up Christmas List

64 Hard Candy Christmas

68 Here Comes Santa Claus (Right Down Santa Claus Lane)

70 A Holly Jolly Christmas

73 I Saw Mommy Kissing Santa Claus

76 I Still Believe in Santa Claus

80 I Wish Everyday Could Be Like Christmas

84 I'll Be Home for Christmas

87 It's Beginning to Look Like Christmas

90 Jingle-Bell Rock

96 Let It Be Christmas

100 Little Saint Nick

93 Merry Christmas, Darling

104 Merry Christmas Waltz

107 Mister Santa

110 A New York Christmas

118 Nuttin' for Christmas

122 Rockin' Around the Christmas Tree

128 Rudolph the Red-Nosed Reindeer

132 Santa Baby

125 Santa Claus Is Comin' to Town

136 Santa, Bring My Baby Back (To Me)

139 Suzy Snowflake

142 This Christmas

146 When Santa Claus Gets Your Letter

149 You're All I Want for Christmas

BLUE CHRISTMAS

Words and Music by BILLY HAYES
and JAY JOHNSON

Moderately

I'll have a blue Christ-mas, with-out you._____ I'll be so

blue think-ing a-bout you._____ Dec-o-ra-tions of

red on a green Christ-mas tree won't mean a thing if

BRAZILIAN SLEIGH BELLS

By PERCY FAITH

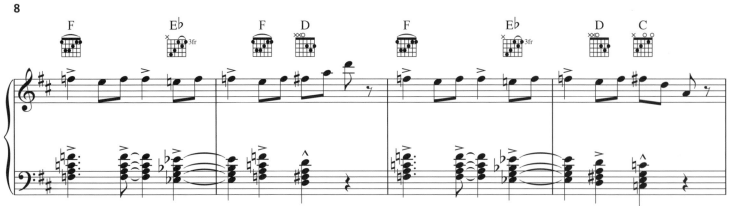

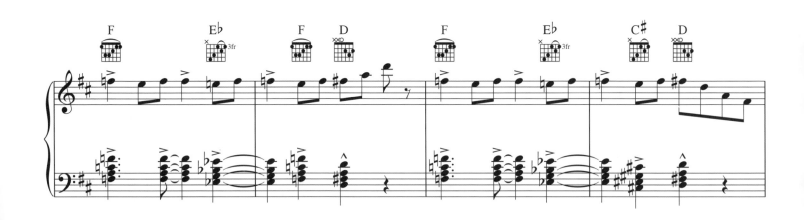

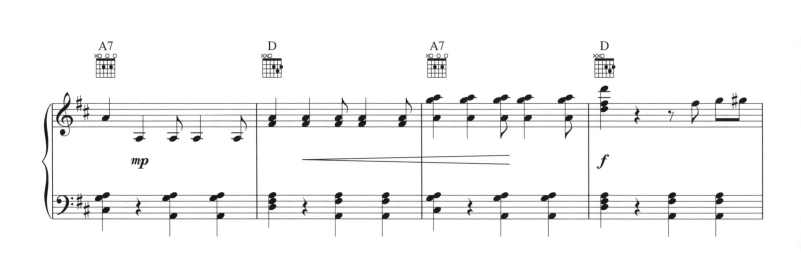

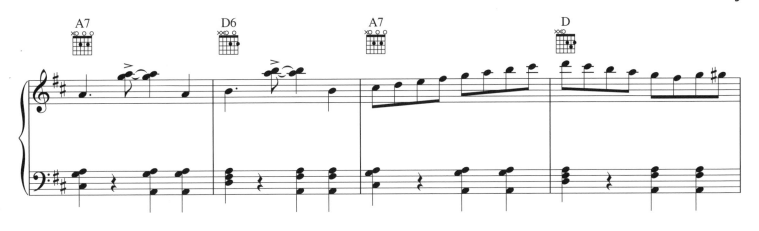

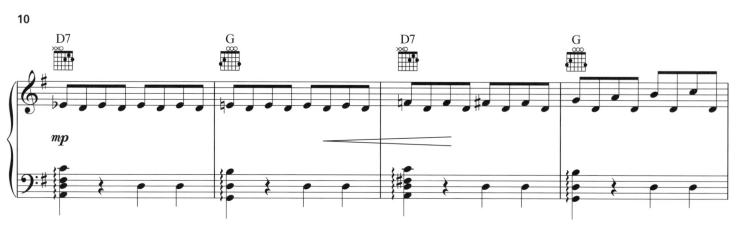

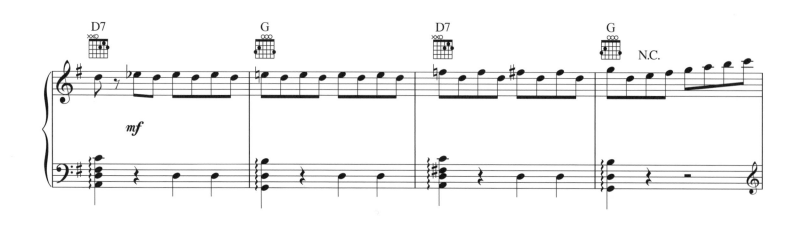

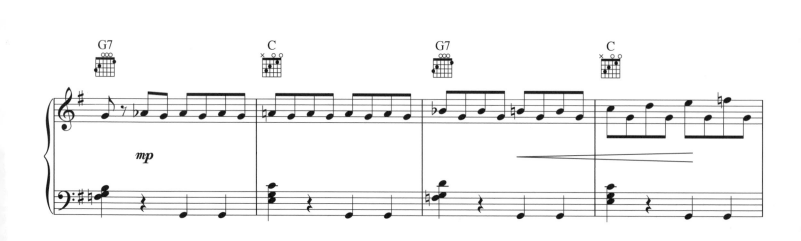

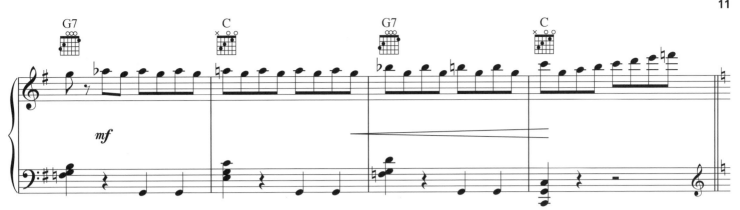

CHRISTMAS DAY

Lyric by HAL DAVID
Music by BURT BACHARACH

CAROLING, CAROLING

Words by WIHLA HUTSON
Music by ALFRED BURT

THE CHIPMUNK SONG

Words and Music by
ROSS BAGDASARIAN

CHRISTMAS IS

Lyrics by SPENCE MAXWELL
Music by PERCY FAITH

A CHRISTMAS MEMORY

Words and Music by
LOONIS McGLOHON

CHRISTMAS TIME IS HERE

from A CHARLIE BROWN CHRISTMAS

Words by LEE MENDELSON
Music by VINCE GUARALDI

29

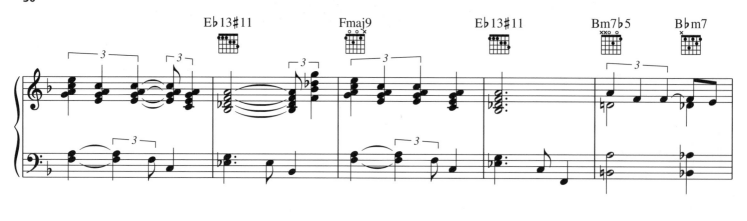

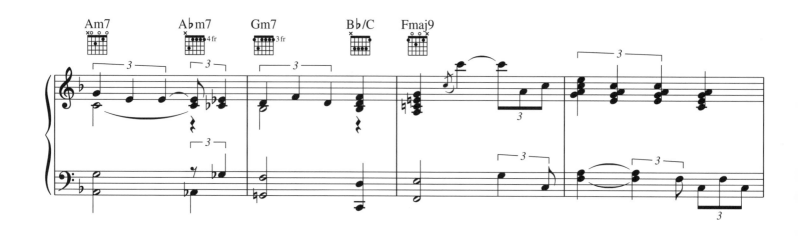

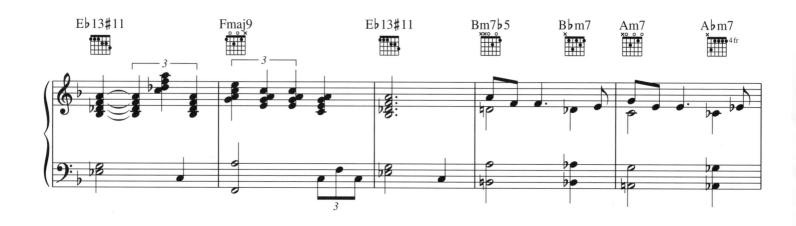

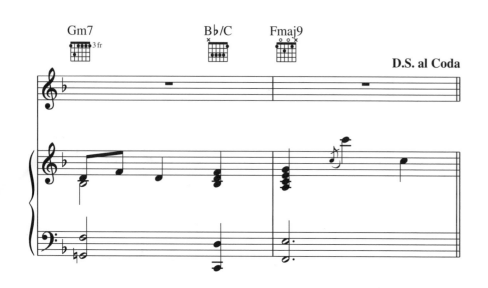

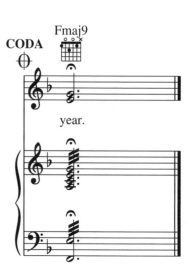

DO YOU HEAR WHAT I HEAR

Words and Music by NOEL REGNEY
and GLORIA SHAYNE

FEELS LIKE CHRISTMAS

Words and Music by PAM WENDELL
and ELMO SHROPSHIRE

FROSTY THE SNOW MAN

Words and Music by STEVE NELSON
and JACK ROLLINS

GIVE THANKS

Words and Music by
CORI CONNORS

GOD BLESS MY FAMILY

Words and Music by
ANN HAMPTON CALLAWAY

It's __ Christ-mas time;
by, the carols we sang as chil - dren __ gath er

out - side, the snow is fall - ing __ like a

mil - lion stars, like a mil - lion dreams all dressed up in white. I'm writ - ing Christ - mas
mem - o - ries. What was just a song now feels like a prayer, wel - com - ing us

cards, a joy that's tinged with sad - ness __ as I think of friends. Some are
home to fa - thers, moth - ers, sis - ters, __ broth - ers ev - 'ry - where. Some we've

GRANDMA'S SPENDING CHRISTMAS WITH THE SUPERSTARS

Words and Music by ELMO SHROPSHIRE
and RITA ABRAMS

Grand - ma's spend - ing Christ - mas with the su - per - stars _____ since that

rein - deer ran her down _____ that fate - ful night. _____

Grand - ma's hang - ing out _____ with all _____ those late, great stars for the

to a ___ new Cad - il - lac, well a, well a, and a
thing sounds ___ just su - per; *(Spoken:) but I'm just*

cou - ple of sheets ___ of El - vis post - age stamps. ___
glad it didn't hit till I was gone!"

1.,2. Grand - ma's spend - ing Christ - mas with the su - per - stars ___ since that
3. *(See additional lyrics)*

rein - deer ran her down ___ that fate - ful night. ___

Grand - ma's hang - ing out ___ with all ___ those late, great stars for the heav - en - li - est Christ - mas of her life. ___

Additional Lyrics

Spoken: Oh, look! Grandma's trying to comb someone's hair. Why, it's Bob Marley!
And look here — she's giving Howard Hughes a manicure!
Oh, poor Richard Burton! She just gave him the news about Elizabeth Taylor Fortensky!

GROWN-UP CHRISTMAS LIST

Words and Music by DAVID FOSTER
and LINDA THOMPSON-JENNER

HARD CANDY CHRISTMAS

Words and Music by
CAROL HALL

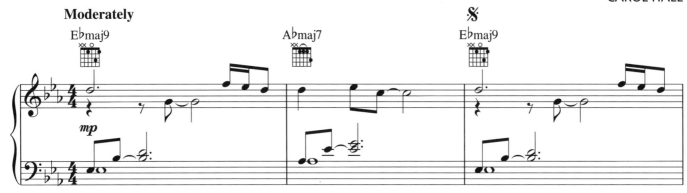

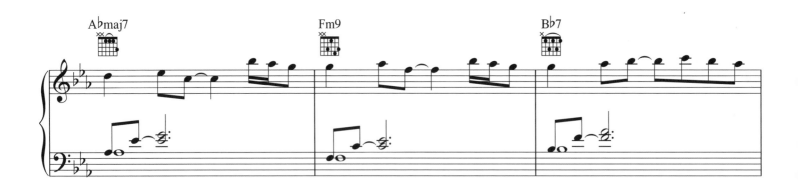

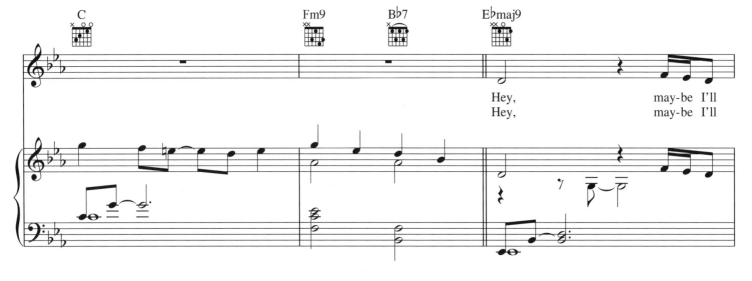

Hey,   may-be I'll
Hey,   may-be I'll

dye   my   hair,   may-be I'll move   some-where.   May-be I'll
learn   to   sew,   may-be I'll just   lie   low.   May-be I'll

HERE COMES SANTA CLAUS
(Right Down Santa Claus Lane)

Words and Music by GENE AUTRY
and OAKLEY HALDEMAN

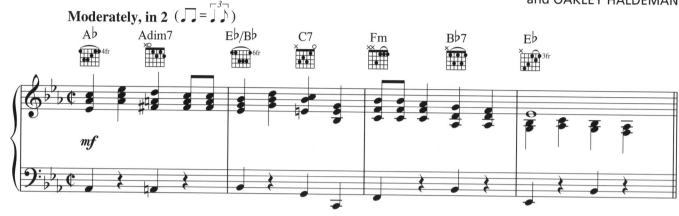

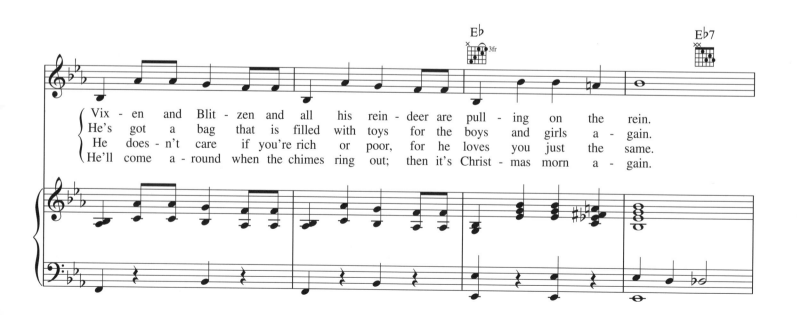

Here comes San - ta Claus! Here comes San - ta Claus! Right down San - ta Claus Lane!

Vix - en and Blitz - en and all his rein - deer are pull - ing on the rein.
He's got a bag that is filled with toys for the boys and girls a - gain.
He does - n't care if you're rich or poor, for he loves you just the same.
He'll come a - round when the chimes ring out; then it's Christ - mas morn a - gain.

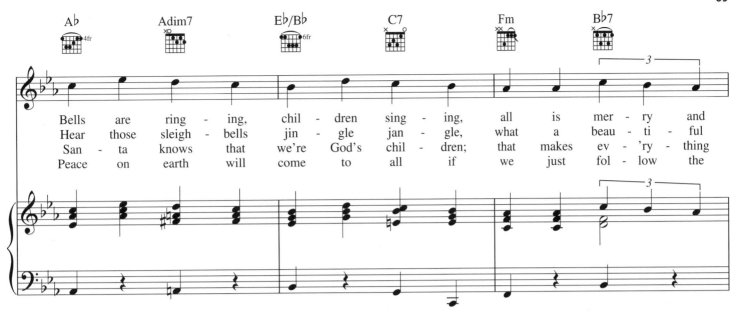

Bells are ring - ing, chil - dren sing - ing, all is mer - ry and
Hear those sleigh - bells jin - gle jan - gle, what a beau - ti - ful
San - ta knows that we're God's chil - dren; that makes ev - 'ry - thing
Peace on earth will come to all if we just fol - low the

bright.
sight. } Hang your stock - ings and say your pray'rs,
right. Jump in bed, cov - er up your head,
light. Fill your hearts with a Christ - mas cheer, } 'cause
Let's give thanks to the Lord a - bove,

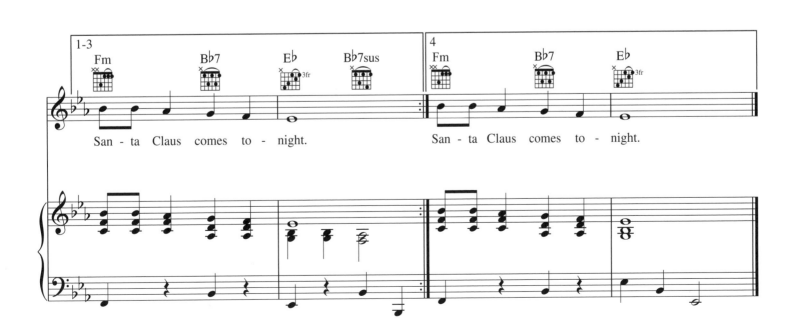

San - ta Claus comes to - night.
San - ta Claus comes to - night.

A HOLLY JOLLY CHRISTMAS

Music and Lyrics by
JOHNNY MARKS

I SAW MOMMY KISSING SANTA CLAUS

Words and Music by
TOMMIE CONNOR

I STILL BELIEVE IN SANTA CLAUS

Words and Music by MAURICE STARR
and AL LANCELLOTTI

I WISH EVERYDAY COULD BE LIKE CHRISTMAS

Words and Music by DAVID ERWIN
and JIM CARTER

I'LL BE HOME FOR CHRISTMAS

Words and Music by KIM GANNON
and WALTER KENT

Moderately slow

I'm dream-ing to-night of a place I love, __ e-ven more than I u-sual-ly do. And al-though I know it's a long road back, __ I prom-ise you

IT'S BEGINNING TO LOOK LIKE CHRISTMAS

By MEREDITH WILLSON

JINGLE-BELL ROCK

Words and Music by JOE BEAL
and JIM BOOTHE

MERRY CHRISTMAS, DARLING

Words and Music by RICHARD CARPENTER
and FRANK POOLER

Greet-ing cards have all been sent, the Christ-mas rush is through,

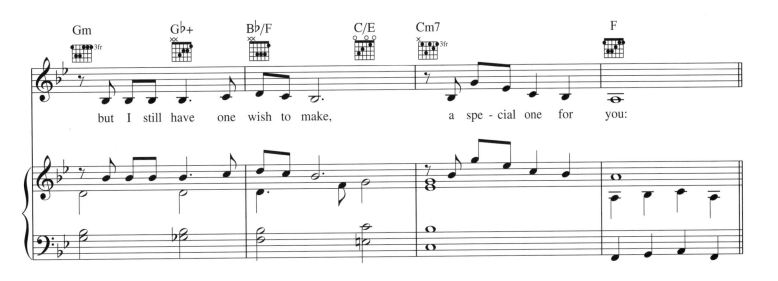

but I still have one wish to make, a spe-cial one for you:

Mer-ry Christ-mas, dar-ling. We're a-part, that's true; but

LET IT BE CHRISTMAS

Words and Music by
ALAN JACKSON

LITTLE SAINT NICK

Words and Music by BRIAN WILSON
and MIKE LOVE

*Recorded a half step lower.

MERRY CHRISTMAS WALTZ

Words and Music by BOB BATSON
and INEX LOEWER

MISTER SANTA

Words and Music by
PAT BALLARD

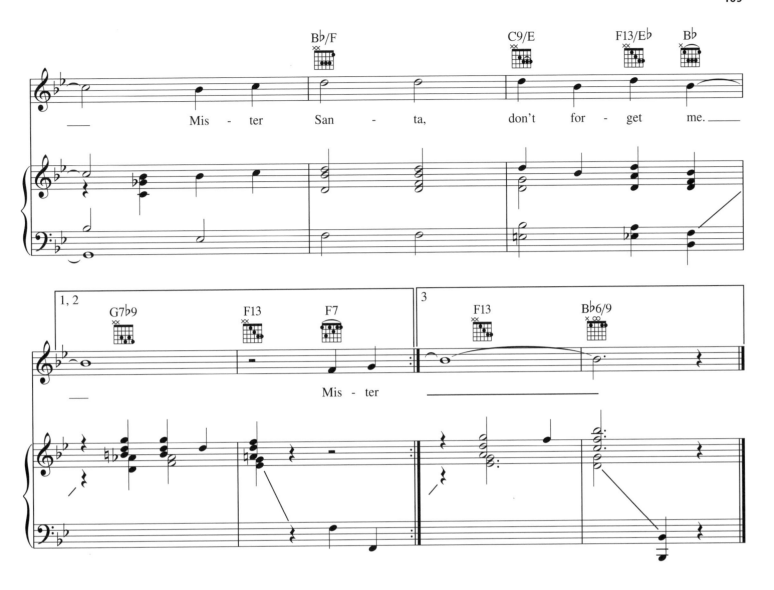

Additional Lyrics

2. Mister Santa, dear old Saint Nick,
Be awful careful and please don't get sick.
Put on your coat when breezes are blowin',
And when you cross the street look where you're goin'.
Santa, we (I) love you so,
We (I) hope you never get lost in the snow.
Take your time when you unpack,
Mister Santa, don't hurry back.

3. Mister Santa, we've been so good;
We've washed the dishes and done what we should.
Made up the beds and scrubbed up our toesies,
We've used a kleenex when we've blown our nosesies.
Santa, look at our ears, they're clean as whistles,
We're sharper than shears.
Now we've put you on the spot,
Mister Santa, bring us a lot.

A NEW YORK CHRISTMAS

Words and Music by
ROB THOMAS

*Recorded a half step higher.

114

NUTTIN' FOR CHRISTMAS

Words and Music by ROY BENNETT
and SID TEPPER

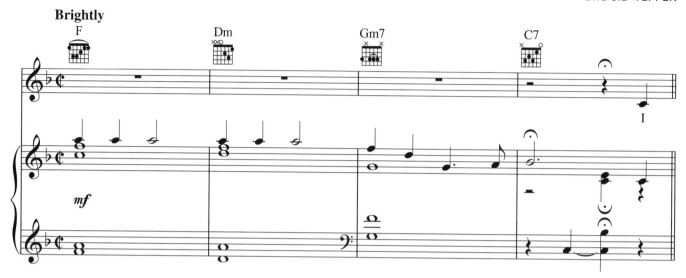

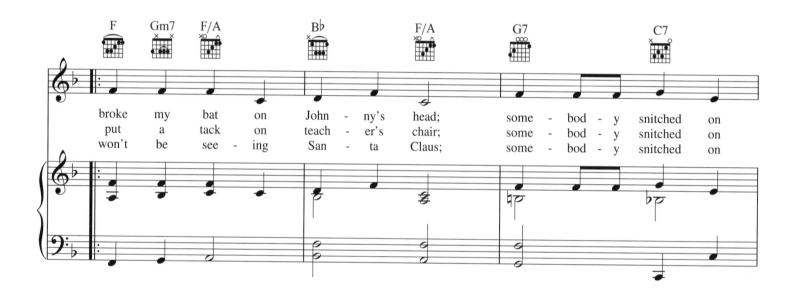

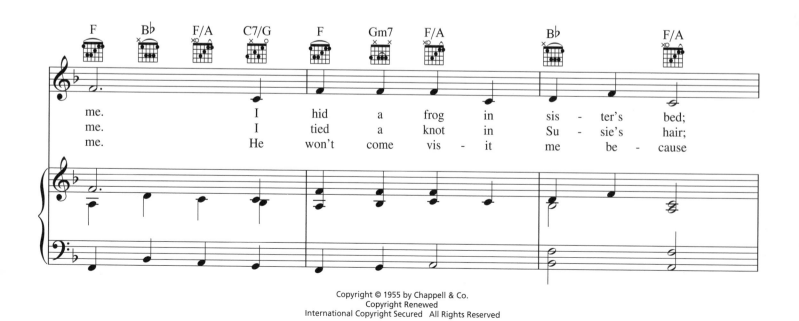

ROCKIN' AROUND THE CHRISTMAS TREE

Music and Lyrics by
JOHNNY MARKS

SANTA CLAUS IS COMIN' TO TOWN

Words by HAVEN GILLESPIE
Music by J. FRED COOTS

Lyrics:
You bet-ter watch out, you bet-ter not cry, bet-ter not pout, I'm tell-ing you why: San-ta Claus is com-in' to town. He's

RUDOLPH THE RED-NOSED REINDEER

Music and Lyrics by
JOHNNY MARKS

SANTA BABY

By JOAN JAVITS,
PHIL SPRINGER and TONY SPRINGER

SANTA, BRING MY BABY BACK
(To Me)

Words and Music by CLAUDE DeMETRUIS
and AARON SCHROEDER

SUZY SNOWFLAKE

Words and Music by SID TEPPER
and ROY BENNETT

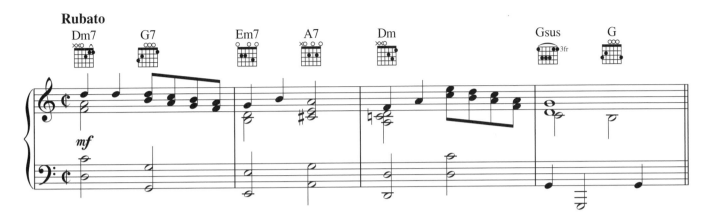

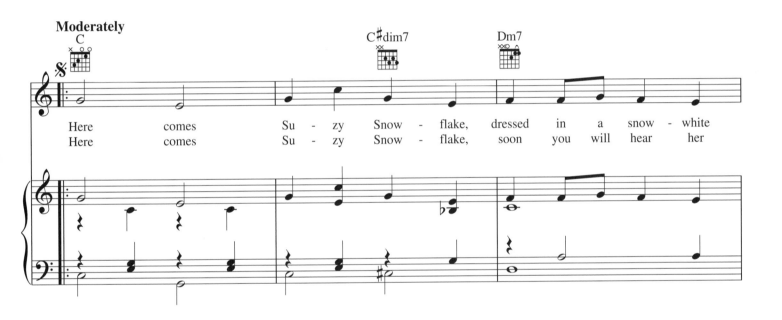

Here comes Suzy Snowflake, dressed in a snow-white
Here comes Suzy Snowflake, soon you will hear her

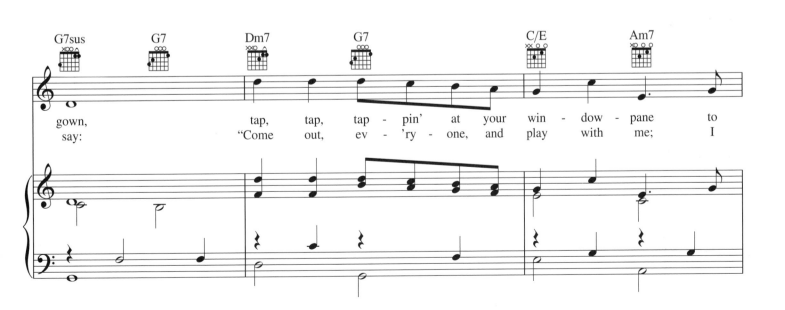

gown, tap, tap, tap-pin' at your win-dow-pane to
say: "Come out, ev-'ry-one, and play with me; I

THIS CHRISTMAS

Words and Music by DONNY HATHAWAY
and NADINE McKINNOR

(1.,4.) Hang all the mis-tle-toe.__ I'm gon-na get to know you bet-ter __
(2.) Pres-ents and cards are here.__ My world is filled with cheer and you, _____
(3.) *Piano solo ad lib.*

WHEN SANTA CLAUS GETS YOUR LETTER

Music and Lyrics by
JOHNNY MARKS

YOU'RE ALL I WANT FOR CHRISTMAS

Words and Music by GLEN MOORE
and SEGER ELLIS

When San-ta comes a-round at Christ-mas time and leaves a lot of cheer at ev-'ry door, if he would on-ly grant the wish in my heart

Christmas Collections
From Hal Leonard
All books arranged for piano, voice, & guitar.

Christmas Time Is Here

A 50-song Christmas collection! Includes: As Long as There's Christmas • Caroling, Caroling • The Christmas Song • Christmas Time Is Here • Do You Hear What I Hear • Emmanuel • Feliz Navidad • Let's Make It Christmas All Year 'Round • The Most Wonderful Time of the Year • Santa Baby • Silver Bells • and more!
00310761 ....$16.95

The Best Christmas Songs Ever - 3rd Edition

A collection of more than 70 of the best-loved songs of the season, including: Blue Christmas • Frosty the Snow Man • Grandma Got Run Over by a Reindeer • I'll Be Home for Christmas • Jingle-Bell Rock • Rudolph, The Red-Nosed Reindeer • Silver Bells • You're All I Want for Christmas • and many more.
00359130 ....$19.95

The Big Book Of Christmas Songs

An outstanding collection of over 120 all-time Christmas favorites and hard-to-find classics. Features: Angels We Have Heard on High • As Each Happy Christmas • Auld Lang Syne • The Boar's Head Carol • Christ Was Born on Christmas Day • Bring a Torch Jeannette, Isabella • Carol of the Bells • Coventry Carol • Deck the Halls • The First Noel • The Friendly Beasts • God Rest Ye Merry Gentlemen • I Heard the Bells on Christmas Day • It Came Upon a Midnight Clear • Jesu, Joy of Man's Desiring • Joy to the World • Masters in This Hall • O Holy Night • The Story of the Shepherd • 'Twas the Night Before Christmas • What Child Is This? • and many more. Includes guitar chord frames.
00311520 ....$19.95

Season's Greetings

A great big collection of 50 favorites, including: All I Want for Christmas Is You • Blue Christmas • The Christmas Song • Frosty the Snow Man • Grandma Got Run Over by a Reindeer • Happy Holiday • I'll Be Home for Christmas • Most of All I Wish You Were Here • Silver Bells • What Made the Baby Cry? • and more.
00310426 ....$16.95

Christmas Songs For Kids

27 songs kids love to play during the holidays, including: Away in a Manger • The Chipmunk Song • Deck the Hall • The First Noel • Jingle Bells • Joy to the World • O Christmas Tree • Silent Night • and more.
00311571 ....$7.95

Contemporary Christian Christmas

20 songs as recorded by today's top Christian artists, including: Michael W. Smith (All Is Well) • Sandi Patty (Bethlehem Morning) • Amy Grant (Breath of Heaven) • Michael Card (Celebrate the Child) • Steven Curtis Chapman (Going Home for Christmas) • Michael English (Mary Did You Know?) • Steve Green (Rose of Bethlehem) • 4Him (A Strange Way to Save the World) • Point of Grace (This Gift) • Scott Wesley Brown (This Little Child) • and more.
00310643 ....$12.95

The Definitive Christmas Collection – 2nd Edition

All the Christmas songs you need in one convenient collection! Over 120 classics in all! Songs include: An Old Fashioned Christmas • Away in a Manger • The Chipmunk Song • Christmas Time Is Here • The Christmas Waltz • Do They Know It's Christmas • Feliz Navidad • The First Noel • Frosty the Snow Man • The Greatest Gift of All • Happy Holiday • A Holly Jolly Christmas • I Saw Mommy Kissing Santa Claus • Jingle-Bell Rock • Mister Santa • My Favorite Things • O Holy Night • Rudolph, The Red-Nosed Reindeer • Santa, Bring My Baby Back (To Me) • Silent Night • Silver Bells • Suzy Snowflake • We Need a Little Christmas • and many more.
00311602 ....$29.95

The Lighter Side of Christmas

42 fun festive favorites, including: Grandma Got Run Over by a Reindeer • A Holly Jolly Christmas • I Guess There Ain't No Santa Claus • I Saw Mommy Kissing Santa Claus • Jingle-Bell Rock • The Merry Christmas Polka • Rockin' Around the Christmas Tree • Rudolph the Red-Nosed Reindeer • That's What I'd Like for Christmas • and more.
00310628 ....$14.95

Ultimate Christmas - 3rd Edition

100 seasonal favorites, including: Auld Lang Syne • Bring a Torch, Jeannette, Isabella • Carol of the Bells • The Chipmunk Song • Christmas Time Is Here • The First Noel • Frosty the Snow Man • Gesù Bambino • Happy Holiday • Happy Xmas (War Is Over) • Hymne • Jesu, Joy of Man's Desiring • Jingle-Bell Rock • March of the Toys • My Favorite Things • The Night Before Christmas Song • Pretty Paper • Silver and Gold • Silver Bells • Suzy Snowflake • What Child Is This • The Wonderful World of Christmas • and more.
00361399 ....$19.95